A CHILD'S BOOK OF
OLD NURSERY RHYMES

A CHILD'S BOOK OF

Old

Nursery

Rhymes

JOAN WALSH ANGLUND

A Margaret K. McElderry Book

Atheneum   1973   New York

Copyright © 1973 by Joan Walsh Anglund
All rights reserved
Library of Congress catalog card number 73-75429
ISBN 0-689-30413-7
Published simultaneously in Canada by
McClelland & Stewart, Ltd.
Manufactured in the United States of America
Printed by Connecticut Printers, Inc., Hartford
Bound by A. Horowitz & Son/Bookbinders
Clifton, New Jersey
First Edition

I love little Pussy,
    Her coat is so warm;
And if I don't hurt her,
    She'll do me no harm.

So I'll not pull her tail,
    Nor drive her away;
But Pussy and I
    Very gently will play.

Little Boy Blue,
  Come blow your horn!
The sheep's in the meadow,
  The cow's in the corn.

Where is the little boy
  Who looks after the sheep?
He's under the haystack
  Fast asleep.

One ... two,
  Buckle my shoe.

Three ... four,
  Close the door.

Five ... six,
  Pick up sticks.

Rain, rain, go away,
  Come again another day,
Little Emily wants to play.

Polly, put the kettle on,
    Polly, put the kettle on ;
Polly, put the kettle on,
    And we'll all have tea.

A dillar, a dollar,
   A ten o'clock scholar,
What makes you come so soon?
   You used to come at ten o'clock,
But now you come at noon.

One foot up
    And one foot down;
That's the way
    To London town.

Knock at the door!
Peep in!
Lift up the latch!
And walk in!

(a baby's face)

Purple, yellow, red and green,
The King cannot reach it,
nor can the Queen.

(a rainbow)

Little Nancy Etticoat
   In a white petticoat
And a red nose;
   The longer she stands,
The shorter she grows.

(a candle)

As round as an apple,
   As deep as a cup,
And all the King's horses
   Cannot pull it up.

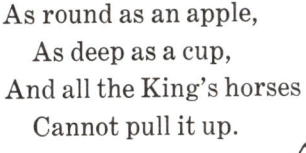

(a well)

Hush baby, my doll,
  I pray you don't cry;
And I'll give you some bread
  And some milk by and by.
Perhaps you'd like cake,
  Or maybe a tart;
Then to either you're welcome
  With all of my heart.

Pat-a-cake, pat-a-cake,
    Baker's man,
Bake me a cake,
    As fast as you can.

Pat it and roll it,
    And mark it with a B,
And put it in the oven,
    For baby and me.

Mary had a little lamb,
  Its fleece was white as snow;
And everywhere that Mary went,
  The lamb was sure to go.

It followed her to school one day,
  Which was against the rule;
It made the children laugh and play,
  To see a lamb at school.

And so the teacher turned it out,
  But still it lingered near;
And waited patiently about,
  'Til Mary did appear.

What makes the lamb love Mary so?
  The children they did cry;
Why Mary loves the lamb you know,
  The teacher did reply.

Rock-a-bye, baby, on the tree top,
When the wind blows,
        the cradle will rock;
When the bough breaks,
        the cradle will fall,
And down will come baby,
        cradle and all.

Little Miss Muffet
　Sat on a tuffet,
Eating her curds and whey;
　Along came a spider
And sat down beside her
　And frightened Miss Muffet away.

Little Jack Horner
>   sat in the corner,
Eating his Christmas pie;

He put in his thumb,
>   and pulled out a plum,
And said,
>   "What a good boy am I!"

The north wind doth blow
   And we shall have snow,
And what will poor Robin do then?
   Poor thing!

He'll sit in the barn,
   And keep himself warm,
And hide his head under his wing.
   Poor thing!

Hey, diddle, diddle!
The cat and the fiddle,

The cow jumped
over the moon;

The little dog laughed
to see such sport,

And the dish
ran away
with the spoon.

Mary, Mary, quite contrary,
 How does your garden grow?
With silver bells and cockle-shells,
 And pretty maids all in a row.

London Bridge is falling down,
Falling down, falling down;
London Bridge is falling down,
My fair lady.

See-saw, Margery Daw,
    Jenny shall have a new master;
She shall earn but a penny a day,
    Because she can't work any faster.

Star light, star bright,
   First star I see tonight;

I wish I may, I wish I might
   Have the wish I wish tonight.

Diddle diddle dumpling,
  My son John,
Went to bed with his trousers on,
  One shoe off, and the other shoe on;
Diddle diddle dumpling, my son John.

The Man in the Moon
>	looked out of the moon,
And this is what he said,
" 'Tis time that, now I'm getting up,
All children went to bed."